A Note to Parents and

DK READERS is a compelling reading programme for children, designed in conjunction with leading literacy experts, including Cliff Moon M.Ed., Honorary Fellow of the University of Reading. Cliff Moon has spent many years as a teacher and teacher educator specializing in reading and has written more than 160 books for children and teachers. He is series editor to Collins Big Cat.

Beautiful illustrations and superb full-colour photographs combine with engaging, easy-to-read stories to offer a fresh approach to each subject in the series. Each DK READER is guaranteed to capture a child's interest while developing his or her reading skills, general knowledge, and love of reading.

The five levels of DK READERS are aimed at different reading abilities, enabling you to choose the books that are exactly right for your child:

Pre-level 1: Learning to read
Level 1: Beginning to read
Level 2: Beginning to read alone
Level 3: Reading alone
Level 4: Proficient readers

The "normal" age at which a child begins to read can be anywhere from three to eight years old, so these levels are only a general guideline.

No matter which level you select, you can be sure that you are helping your child learn to read, then read to learn!

LONDON, NEW YORK, MUNICH,
MELBOURNE, and DELHI

Series Editors Deborah Lock,
Penny Smith
Art Editor Clare Shedden
Production Angela Graef
DTP Designer Almudena Díaz
Jacket Designer Hedi Gutt
Picture Researcher Liz Moore

Reading Consultant
Cliff Moon, M.Ed.

Published in Great Britain by
Dorling Kindersley Limited
80 Strand, London WC2R ORL
6 8 10 9 7
011-DD342-06/2006
A Penguin Company

A CIP record for this book is available
from the British Library

ISBN-13: 978-1-4053-1499-2

Colour reproduction by Colourscan, Singapore
Printed and bound in China by L Rex Printing Co., Ltd.

The publisher would like to thank the following for their kind
permission to reproduce their photographs:
a=above; c=centre; b=below; l=left; r=right; t=top

Alamy/Enigma: 7t, Paul Sterry 31tr; **Ardea:** Brian Bevan
14-15, 32ca background, 18-19, John Cancalosi 11cl, John
Daniels 9c, 32tl, Steve Hopkin 12-13, 23, John Clegg
27; **Corbis:** D. Robert Franz 3, Gabe Palmer 4, Ron Sanford
10t; **Getty Images:** Stuart McCall 8t, Photodisc Blue-Bruce
Heinemann 30-31; **Image State:** Premium Stock 28-29; **Nature
Picture Library:** Martin Dohrn 24c, 32cb, Adrian Davies 30-
31c; **Science Photo Library:** Pat & Tom Leeson 6t.
All other images © Dorling Kindersley
For more information see: www.dkimages.com

Discover more at
www.dk.com

Contents

LEARNING
pre-level
1
TO READ

Duck Pond Dip

DK
A Dorling Kindersley Book

duck pond

Let's visit
the duck pond.

Ducks splash
in the duck pond.

splash

 ducks

ducklings

Ducklings paddle
in the duck pond.

paddle

Geese honk in the duck pond.

gosling

 geese

Honk!

Frogs croak
in the duck pond.

frogs

eye

Croak!
Croak!

tadpoles

14

Tadpoles wriggle
in the duck pond.

tail

Newts swim
in the duck pond.

newts

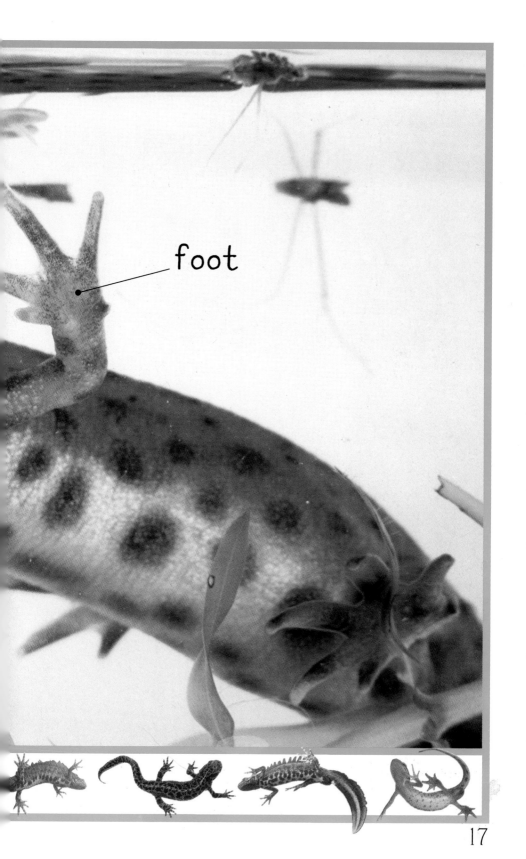

foot

Fish swim in the duck pond.

fish

fin

shell

snails

Snails crawl
in the duck pond.

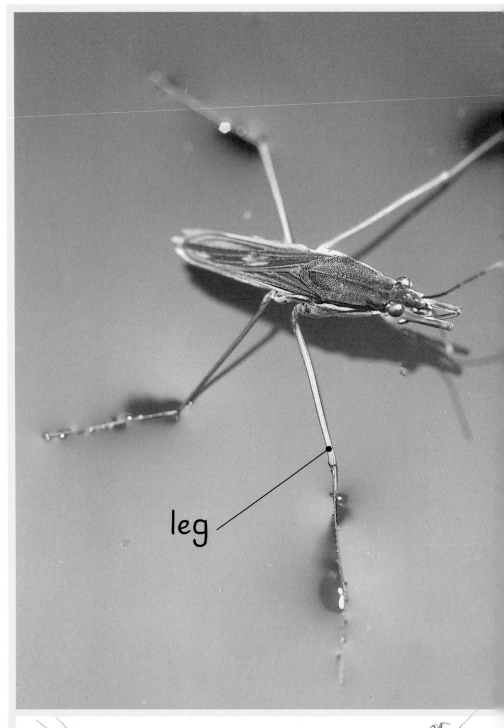

leg

 water boatmen

Water boatmen walk
on the duck pond.

Dragonflies fly over the duck pond.

dragonflies

wing

antenna

Beetles dive
in the duck pond.

beetles

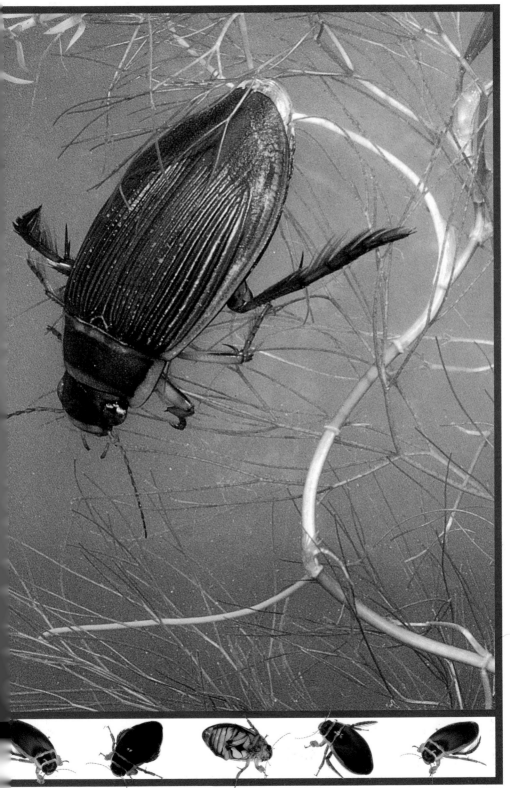

Mosquitoes buzz over the duck pond.

 mosquitoes

head

What else do you see?

heron

water lily

kingfisher

pondweed

bulrushes

Glossary

Duckling a young duck

Tadpoles baby frogs

Water boatman an insect that can walk on water

Dragonfly a flying insect that lives by water

Water lily a flower that grows in water